THE MAN IN THE MIRROR

A POEM COLLECTION ON MALE MENTAL HEALTH

By Chris Statham

Also By

THE UGLY GLORY SERIES

THE MAN IN THE MIRROR - A collection on male mental health
FRIDAY NIGHT FEVER – A collection on booze, nightlife & the battle with sobriety
JELLIED EELS & MULTI-CULTURALISM – A collection on modern life in the UK
THIS IS WHY WE MET - A collection on dating, friends with benefits & sex workers
MY NORTH STAR - A collection on love, divorce & finding a way forward
JUST ANOTHER MARTIAN CAT LIVING IN BASILDON - A collection on exploring creativity & the world
LIFE PRIRATE – A collection on life, death & all that jazz

AFRONIA SERIES

Crying for Afronia (Volume 1)
Escape from Afronia (Volume 2)
Dying for Afronia (Volume 3)
Afronia Rising (Volume 4)
Developing Afronia (Volume 5)

PROSE, POEM AND PICTURES SERIES

7 Days in 1 Week (Volume 1)
12 Months in a Year (Volume 2)
10 Years in a Decade (Volume 3)

OTHER FICTION NOVELS

18 Reflections and 3 Statements of Relief
Paperback Writer

DEDICATION

To Darren, Maron, Geordie and other good listerners

Copyright and Disclaimer

Author – Chris Statham
Sketches by Hezdean Chinthengah
Published by **www.creativityxroads.com**
The Man in the Mirror, 978-1-9989924-7-8

CONTENTS

FORWARD

I empathize with the complexity and challenges you're currently facing as a man; life has never seem so confusing, bewildering. My world around me is crumbling. My father passed away last month, I've started my divorce after 14 years of marriage, work is slowing down and debt going up; it's all quite bleak, a bit shitty. Uncertainty looms. I don't know what access I will have to my 4 kids or my future financial responsibilities. It's very depressing. I have a lot going on in my head, and yet if I talk too much someone will accuse me of having emotional man flu.

Until recently, I had a relatively easy ride in life. But, when I look around and digest the joint cultural influences of celebrity and social media, I see a distorted image of the good life rather than the reality for many boys and men. This, I believe, lies at the root of the male mental health crisis. The stereotype of men being tough emotionally closed-off and only seeking connection when wanting sex is very limited. The reality for many boys and men, we underachieve at school and are less likely to go into further education compared with girls. We are more likely to become addicted to drugs, alcohol and pornography. Men make up the majority of suicides, being homeless, being in prison, being in gangs, being unemployed and dying at work, being murdered. Heartbreakingly, men are in the majority of those who lose custody of their children in divorce. It's no wonder there is a male mental health crisis!

I accept my responsibilities as a father, but also want to put my past behind and move on... but societal expectations as a man, father, and ex-husband mean I chicken out and don't make the changes in my life that I need. I keep to the repetitive cycle of waking at seven, going to work, return from work, drink tillI'm unconscious, my emotions numbed and then do it all again the next day... and for some reason expect an outcome different to being utterly unfulfilled.

I have reached out to The Samaritans, friends and therapists to gain a deeper understanding of who I am, and what I need to do to get through this exceptionally tough part of my life as I try to forge a sustainable way forward. Writing poems has helped me better understand my core beliefs and how they are in conflict with my sub-conscious; its a challenging mental landscape, or to put it another way, a mind-fuck.

Navigating this complex journey, I have organised my poems into different themes to understand and shed light on the challenges, I, and expect many men and boys are facing. I am brutally honest, this to break taboos and start conversations around male mental health. I start with trying to understand who I am and where I fit into this extremely confusing world. How, at times, this becomes overwhelming, the constant flux of internal conflict triggering ugly thoughts. However, ultimately, I've come to realise, I'm the only person who can get me out of the funk.

I now know, reaching out for support and understanding is an act of strength, a willingness to explore and confront your issues. So, I say, keep seeking the path that leads to healing, self-discovery and a more fulfilling life. And, if someone reaches out to you, be a good listneer and friend.

WHO AM I?

Gender roles and expectations have undergone significant transformation over the years, equality now the guiding principle. Generation X was brought up on the notion of joint family responsibility rather than the stereotype of male breadwinners and female homemakers. This has not turned out to be the reality. In past generations, women were supposed to be cake bakers, child factories and sexual tigresses to the whims of their husbands; the man for his part earned. Now, men don't have a definitive answer to the question, what is it to be male? The mass media gives conflicting messages about masculinity. On the one hand, that to be a man you have to be a reliable earner, to pump iron, be dominant and sexually assertive and take care of your appearance, and on the other, change nappies and stroll with the pushchair around the park. Modern men find themselves grappling with the question, what does it truly means to be male?

I think masculinity and femininity are daft, arbitrary stereotypes. What does it truly mean if someone says, that bloke is (or isn't) a man? What or who is a man's man? Is it the ability to stoically keep emotions in check? An inability to express vulnerability but rather keep a stiff upper lip? Your ability to close your heart and not cry in front of others? Drink 20 pints and fuck 3 girls in the same night? These are one-dimensional definitions of manhood. It's a bit like saying, all men like football or, to be a man you must be able to bench press 100 kilograms. I think the difference between men and women it just a few lose bits of skin, and then it comes down to character, emotions, friendships and good stuff like that.

Men often struggle to answer questions, such as, are you ok or, what's the matter? We mumble a reply, yet, if we're asked, what's the score or fancy a pint? we can wax lyrically even though this does us no good. It is a very confusing time to be a man, expectations seemingly changing by the day. Ultimately, life, regardless of gender, is the history of lives. The rich tapestry of success stories, weddings, births, jobs, your house is your castle etc. But also, of emotional distress, physical and mental damage, death, divorce, dementia, dismissals.

It's an undeniably confusing time to be a man, expectations shifting constantly, this what the first set of poems is about.

Who and What is a Modern Man?

Males,
sons, brothers, fathers, granddad,
50% of the population,
so many shapes and sizes but all told,
live like a man,
a lion;
hold your head high,
be proud of who you are and what you represent.

To the pride,
we are the figurehead,
the leader,
the clan's champion;
the crown sits on our head,
this our life,
our fate,
our destiny to be the king.

But,
we must compromise our happiness for others,
sacrifice our sexual desires for one lioness,
forget our dreams for a smile on our children's,
a lover's,
a proud parents' face.

As a king,
I have huge responsibility.
I must find my love, my light,
the one to make me happy,
to calm my inner seas so together we conquer the
savannah in a turbulent world.

But, if I see my girl with another man and become
anxious,
women say,
I'm jealous and insecure.
If I remain silent,
men tell me,
man up.

When I'm with the lads,
my woman says I'm unthoughtful,

but if I stay at home I'm lazy.
When my children are naugh-
ty and I tell them off,
I'm uncaring;
if I do nothing,
I'm irresponsible.

We endure scolding from our
mothers,
sarcasm from our wives,
mocking from our children,
castigation from our bosses,
and are quizzed by the bank
manager.

We toil without complaint to ensure bread is on
the table,
that there's a bright future for all.

We keep our financial and mental torments hid-
den.
We lock our heart not letting others know our
pain,
frustrations and loneliness in our struggles.
We never let our smile slip as we try to secure the
future for our pride.

Wives, mothers, sisters, daughters,
know I'm not the cause or solution to all your
problems.
I can't always be your emotional punch bag.
I try my best,
my hardest,
but remember,
I also have my own shit to contend with.

Being a man,
a lion,
a king,
we're pulled in 100 directions –
the crown rarely sitting easily.

Bull Elephant

I am an elephant,
a bull,
the biggest of beasts,
a king that can't be challenged.

No one or thing dares get in my way;
animal, human, tree,
I can crush them all.
This land I own.
I go where I want,
trundle and make love;
time is mine.

I will sleep and eat,
screw when and how I want,
nothing can stop me
destroy me,
disrobe or dethrone my majesty.

But…
when I look in the river,
I see my reflection,
an ant.

My insecurities challenge me,
drown me.

I was born into a position of power…
at the cost of being someone I'm not.
I act rather than being my true self.

I am humble,
quiet,
an individual of rhetorical questions so uncertain
am I.
My ego doesn't match my bulk.
I don't want to live up to expectation of peers,
my ancestors,
parents,
siblings,

community;
I just want to be me.

Mine are the tears of a clown,
no gems coming from me.
It is enough to keep my own head above water,
be the last man in my garrison,
the world imploding around,
my mental health shot while keeping up appear-
ances,
being the man,
the individual others expect me to be,
all the while the hurt inside suffocating,
mesmerising,
debilitating,
I trying,
struggling to surviving,
barley able to get through the day.

Manning Up

Man up,
I'm told;
what does that mean?

Manning up…
is that drinking all night,
fucking like a rabbit,
taking ridiculous risks,
keeping inner torment to myself?

Manning up can be thinking of others,
not needing to be alpha,
rather, a happy confident beta,
knowing what's going on,
happy in own skin,
not needing to prove anything to others.

Manning up,
a nonsense,
an oxymoron.
In life,
your biggest strength is to admit your weaknesses
as then you can find solutions,

learn and adapt,
grow stronger through others' experiences,
success and failures.
I need to get my head in the right space,
place,
then I will be whole,
can do what I need to do for me,
for others…
only then can I say,
I'm man enough that I don't need to confirm to
harmful stereotypes,
that I'm manning up.

Monkey

I read books,
but I'm better at reading my own kind-
my inner man a monkey.

I sit in an office,
a tree a more natural habitat-
my inner man a monkey.

I mainly social on media,
not in my troop-
my inner man a monkey.

I love my spouse,
religion restricting me to one-
my inner man a monkey.

I'm told to man up,
to live my inner monkey-
and then I am castigated for it.
I work to earn money,
Is this surviving?
My inner man a monkey.

I roam the world,
but have no place to call home-
I'm jealous of my inner monkey.

I take more than I need,
defeat my environment-
the MAN overriding his inner monkey.

I do what's not good for my body,
mind or soul-
my inner monkey defeated by the expectations of
modern man

Drained

I am who I am,
usually active,
alive,
electric,
seeing opportunities and joining dots.

A live wire who works hard,
plays harder,
fucks well,
dance on tables and skinny-dips under the
moonlight.

But I'm drained emotionally,
spiritually,
not yet physically,
soon to be financially.

Need a pick-me up,
fuck-me up,
a change of scenery to reignite,
fight not flight,
back up the valley,
new friendships to explore and places to see...

Do I still have that in me?

Not in this place,
not at this time.
I'm done,
mental burn out,
too much stress.

I can't risk more rejection,
dejection,
so keep to myself,
this against all who I am.

For now,
this is the safe option,
I no longer willing to dare,
just wanting to get through the day,
the week,
the... to when something changes,
that brings me out of this funk,
the black dog of depression vanished,
my mind once more free and willing,
ready to take on the world,
reinvigorated,
anticipated,
no longer emotionally constipated.

Loneliness

I sit,
alone,
a quiet trombone,
no brother,
sister or mister to keep me company,
no orchestra of friends,
cacophony of contacts to bide my time with.

I'm cold,
my heart needing a sweater more than my frigid
body,
something,
somebody to keep me sane,
get me back in the game,
help me cross obstacles,
remind me the sun will rise on the morrow.

But,
for now,
I'm alone,
lonely,
single,
a solitary taxi at the rank on a wet November
evening,
a picture of desolation,
depression,
nor sure who,
when or if I will get another customer,
someone to share minutes with,
to break this spell of misery,
utter loneliness.

I don't care if the someone is prince or pauper,
offender or official,
human interaction,
smile or scowl,
better than nothing,
anything to get me out of my glum,
reinvigorate my soul that's been sucked dry.

Is this the real,
authentic me?

My new life,
future reality,
100 percent banality,
what I have to expect?

The environment changing as I grow older,
nothing excites as I sit,
go through the motions.

Where once there was passion,
highs and lows,
this replaced with not giving a shit,
all I crave,
hit after hit.

This is depressing,
depression,
nothing to live for,
no enthusiasm,
life a black canvas,
emotions black paint-
not even paintbrushes.

I've become zombiefied waiting for hours,
days to pass,
time pass,
hoping the next second or minute will bring calamity,
catastrophe,
something to put me out of misery,
for ever,
or shock me out of this stupor.

This is not my natural state of being,
but this who I am now.
Work boring,
with friends, boring,
late nights I no longer bother.
I rather brood,
wallow,
drown in self-pity for the life passing me by.

I know not what I do,
no longer know who I am.
I wander city to city,
bed to bed,
lie to lie,
not sure what the next week,
day or hour will bring;
I, a lonely whale searching the oceans,
desperately calling out to my missing pod.

I no longer have a drive,
a motivation,
a sense of purpose,
a reason to move forward.

I wake,
eat,
sleep,
repeat,
not caring what makes minutes tick away.

I people watch-
individuals,
couples,
families,
friends,
acquaintances old and new chatting,
joking,
laughing,
flirting,
reminiscing,
enjoying each other's company while I consider my
loneliness,
cast adrift from the one I love,

by the one I love,
who no longer loves me.

What fate holds in store,
I and you,
we,
me can't know,
the only certainties,
only I have my back,
the only person I can rely on.

I will not leave or lie to myself,
I will not let myself down.
It is only I that can decide my future,
decide who I share life with,
as I stand,
the last man at the OK Corral shooting till I've
run dry.

Dreams

Dreams,
what do they say about our experiences,
our mental health?
Crazy in a normal world,
the sub-conscious and last cognitive thought,
our brain and creativity
joining dots that don't exist.

A mini-hamburger that eats you.
Attacked on the beach and saved by a shark.
Eating a banana with the king.
Dying in a car crash after sports day.
Going to work and teeth falling out.
Being bullied at school.
Going to work and nothing….
boring.

Dreams,
what do they say about our experiences,
our mental health?
Crazy in a normal world,
the sub-conscious and last cognitive thought,
our brain and creativity
joining dots that don't exist.

Partying with friends,
overdosing,
muff eating,
tits squeezing,
dick sucking,
ass rimming,
drowning,
dry humping.

Dreams,
what do they say about our experiences,

our mental health?
Crazy in a normal world,
the sub-conscious and last cognitive thought,
our brain and creativity
joining dots that don't exist.

A gorilla's hand serving lion's balls.
Going to Tesco to buy two pints of milk and a
Yorkie.
Having a threesome,
one of whom is a relation.
The President knocking on your door holding a
hotdog.
Going to a funeral in a mankini.

Dreams,
what do they say about our experiences,
our mental health?
Crazy in a normal world,
the sub-conscious and last cognitive thought,
our brain and creativity
joining dots that don't exist.

Every Scar has a Story

Every scar has a story,
these 24 are mine.

That one above my eye,
from walking into a door.

My middle finger,
cut on broken glass when drunk.
My thumb,
breaking when misjudging a catch.

Inside my mouth,
mistakenly punched in a nightclub.
They were trying to hit my BFF...
my face got in the way.

My temple,
being robbed on a bus by a gang and getting
knocked out by a bottle.

My big toe,
from standing on broken glass.

My knee,
a sporting operation.

The one on my hand,
from drunkenly tripping into a ditch.

Another one on my forehead,
when my brother threw me head first into a gar-
den wall.

And another on my forehead,
when getting flayed with a handbag chain from an
angry ex-girlfriend;
I was becoming her ex.

My wrist,
from punching a window in a rage.

My longest scar,
on my ankle from falling off a wall;
I have a permanent screw.

These are my body's scars,
a lifetime of war wounds.

But I'm also responsible for causing them.

Mum's Caesarean,
and when she burnt herself baking my birthday
cake.

My big brother's broken arm,
when I put a stick in his spokes.

Dad's cracked elbow falling off a chair when putting shelves up in my bedroom.

But, it's the scars that can't be seen that hurt the
most and run the deepest.

Abi for turning down my marriage proposal.
Lily for divorcing me.
Having no bond with my sibling.
My father's mysterious disappearance.
Losing Jennings to his own hand.
Not holding my daughter every night.
The passing of my son.

Each scar tells a story of my life,
these 24 are mine.

INNER CONFLICT

I try self-reflection and follow the example of the Greek Stoics by taking stock at the end of every day. I find this is a valuable practice as it cultivates mindfulness and helps to maintain perspective. I try not to be irritated by minor trivialities or act angrily to something that's inconsequential, trivial. I will remind myself, that a lot of shit is going to come flying my way, that humanity acts irrationally and, that I shouldn't take random bad stuff personally. Lastly, I remember that I'm made up of billions of molecules with a zillion influences. While these numbers are huge, I'm inconsequential in the infinity of time and space so should not expect things to work out as I planned but be pleasantly surprised if by some miracle they do. I know life is haphazard and I should accept what I'm given rather than be disappointed by what I don't find. I must accept arbitrariness and philosophise that it's unlikely that I'm neither the conductor nor target of random shit. This is a is a profound perspective that allows me to approach life with a philosophical mind-set and to understand my psychological drivers. However, putting these principles into practice is easier said than done. And, there is no shame in loneliness; it is a universal experience. It's not easy; silence is detrimental, a killer. Recognise that we all need support, this a vital part of navigating life's challenges.

Inner Conflict

I am who I am,
me,
complexity of experiences,
desires,
passions,
hopes and fears,
a mix match of friends and family,
culture,
nature and nurture my life's journey.

I can't always explain but do understand some of
my drivers.
Why I simultaneously want stability and
uncertainty,
security and adventure,
family and self,
rigidity and creativity,
crazy and sensible,
extreme and sedate,
family and Tinder date.

Often,
I don't care,
still need to prove a point,

to live with inner conflict,
always running from and to something.

I'm someone who needs understanding and who
will understand you.
I need a listener to my inner conflict,
as I will listen to you.
Will you board my pirate ship of life,
be my partner in crime,
where there are no rights and wrongs,
just living?

Walk of Life

I walk and walk and walk,
I will walk some more.
There's no maximum as I walk,
no answer to questions I can't ask,
no outlet of decisiveness when decisions are so
hellish.

So, I walk and walk and walk,
my mind doing cartwheels,
the endless possibilities of good and bad,
happy or sad,
a thousand in-betweens of not knowing,
a kaleidoscope of possibility,
the rainbow of opportunity,
fortunity,
if only there was a plain option,
a pattern to follow,
something that guaranteed certainty,
liveability,
creativity,
not give a fuckability;
learnability;
life,
a motherfucker of uncertainty!

This is living,
whether loving or giving,

shitting,
pissing,
finding a way for surviving,
better excelling.

We're all on that tightrope,
a hundred,
thousand metres from doom,
emotional more than physical,
spiritual rather than mental,
trying to work it out
as we take the walk of life.

Birthday Blues

I hear the familiar,
raucous happy birthday chants…
for the forty-fifth time.

As I look in the mirror
I see more grey hair,
a bigger belly,
dark rings around once sparkling eyes.

What should I be happy about?
What is there to celebrate…
making it through another 365 days of hell?

In my teens,
the world was my oyster,
responsible only to whims,
extravagancies and eccentricities;
adult temptation in front,
but financially out of reach.

My twenties arrive.
Life is fun, free and full of exploration.
I'm financially independent and have flown the
nest.

I take life in my stride.
Ups and downs,
few responsibilities;
I can choose the destination of my fate.

Thirties.
Age hits,
responsibility hits,
love handles appear;
I'm no longer a carefree and spirited youth.

I have a lovely son,
daughter and wife.
I've never felt so fulfilled,
so castrated;
I have everything I want but no flexibility.

Now I'm 45.
Life is tough,
crap,
nothing straight-forward.

Plans always go awry,
one calamity follows another.
I drift from my children,
my wife now an ex.

Birthdays come and go,
another day crossed from my destiny,
one more emotional bridge crossed,
one year closer to the day I die,
one year closer to peace,
the challenge of life,
one day,
one year less.

When will fate take me?

From yesterday,
to today,
to tomorrow-
little physical change but mental scars build as I
hum my birthday blues.

Insecurities

My parents were good people,
successful in all they did,
loved up…
I don't want the pressure of being admired by my
children.

My father was a hard man to my mum,
to his enemies…
but he was my God and I will fight my way out of
trouble.

My mother was a used woman,
men used her…
as I will use women to disguise and hide my
shame.

I don't feel attractive to those I desire.
I don't have confidence with the fairer sex.
I drink for Dutch courage to approach the object
of my desire and will fuck anybody,
anywhere at any opportunity.

My friends are mainly divorced;
I will not go through that crushing reality again…
so run from loving relationships,
I forever asked,
why can't I commit?

My partner is successful,
life is easy for them,
they, a mate to all…
I have to compete with them so they know I'm
better.
I grew up in poverty and wanted all I could see.
I'm bombarded by constant marketing,
glamourous lives…
I want money,
I need to provide so gamble,
take money from loan sharks…
get in a debt spiral.

My looks and vitality defined who I was,
but age has caught up…
I refuse to accept the dying of the light.

I'm overweight,
my friends and family whippet like.
I hate myself and my body so comfort eat.

I don't know who I am…
so I choose to be a nobody,
a chameleon that blends into the background of
life.

I hate the world,
it is utterly incomprehensible,
totally unfair…
I will hide from it,
run away thru self-hate,
addiction induced oblivion.

We all have insecurities but they don't have to be
destructive,
definitive.

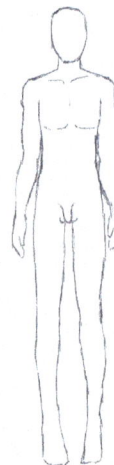

How insecure are you:
- Extremely.
- Yes.
- A little.
- Not at all.
- Definitely not.

My parents were good people,
successful in all they did…
they are role models,
I will strive to be someone my children admire.

My father was a hard man…
but I choose to be a lover not a fighter.

My mother was a prostitute…
I will respect all women.

I don't feel attractive…
but I have an inner strength,
a confidence to chat up those I desire.

My friends divorced…
I will do whatever it takes so my children don't
live the same miserable experience.

My partner is successful…
I will ask for and accept their support.

I grew up in poverty…
and now take entrepreneurship courses.

I don't know who I am…
so will forge an identity and find my motivation,
soul and purpose.

The world is utterly incomprehensible,
not just to me, but for many…
I will help others find their path,
this, part of my life's journey.

My looks and vitality are going…
I will accept age with good grace.

I'm overweight…
so ask friends and family to support my diet and
exercise efforts.

We all have insecurities,
but they don't have to be destructive,
definitive.

I will embrace challenges,
understand my strengths and weaknesses,.
find motivation,
be a free bird and break free of my chains.

Heart of Iron

I advise on big decisions:
follow you heart,
not your brain;
this week,
I have to be made of iron.

There are days in life,
a few,
not many that define who you are.
They reflect the past,
say who you are in the present,
shape the future;
this is one of those weeks.

I advise on big decisions:
follow you heart,
not your brain;
this week,
I have to be made of iron.

This week is life defining,
not just for me but three generations of those I
love,
each impacted,
significantly,
by what I chose,
what conclusion I come to.

I advise on big decisions:
follow you heart,
not your brain;
this week,
I have to be made of iron.

I'll start from smallest to greatest,
easiest to hardest,
the least to most fallout,
the one that is least life-changing,
mind-bending,
limited-contemplating,
heart-breaking.

I advise on big decisions:
follow you heart,
not your brain;
this week,
I have to be made of iron.

12 years a legal case,
about to get ramped-up,
not take a stand up,
time to escalate
negotiate for a lifeline,
is this a financially changing right-time?

I advise on big decisions:
follow you heart,
not your brain;
this week,
I have to be made of iron.

Work decision,
a change of country,
start and end of lives,
no confirmation until contract signation,
this should be regulation,
so far, no completion.

I advise on big decisions:
follow you heart,
not your brain;
this week,
I have to be made of iron.

The hardest,
most ruinous,
most impactful,
a complete motherfucker of a decision,
divorce.

Been married 14 years,
the last 7 not fun,
now time to run.

I still love my wife,
potential for a great life,
she has so much to give,
we have so much in common.

Done my best,
held strong,
four kids not something to walk away from,
mess up.

No bigger life accountability,
the status quo an impossibility,
no longer compatibility,
decision incomparability,
all outcomes shitty.

Have to reach conclusion,
take this hardest of decisions,
like on all other occasions make choices,
accept consequences,
the blame sitting on my head.

I advise on big decisions:
follow you heart,
not your brain;
this week,
I have to be made of iron.

I have not mentioned everything else in my life:
ill parents,
money problems,
struggling to get through the day.

I advise on big decisions:
follow you heart,
not your brain;
this week,
I have to be made of iron.

I wait for confirmation of mind processes,
analyse the course of actions a hundred,
a million times;
this is living on a knife edge,
at the top of the mountain,
precipitous falls either side.

I advise on big decisions:
follow you heart,
not your brain;
this week,
I have to be made of iron.

I must,
will live temet nosce.
Confident in my heart of iron,
remember sisu for obstacles to overcome,
find solutions with meraki,
and understand ikigai,
as,
the greater the challenge the more the man reveals
himself.

In my Element

Being in your element –
but what does this mean?
Attaining a higher state of consciousness?

In love, in music, in sport,
with faith,
there is an inner calm,
when doing what you love,
instinctively knowing:
this is meant to be,
this is my life,
this is my fate –
I am in my element.

I'm bones, blood and soul.
I have dreams and aspirations,
loves and loathes,
but what is my element?

It's not my job where I'm a commodity that can be
hired or fired on whim,
where I sell my soul to the monetary devil as I follow society's rules in misery for tangible trinkets.

I want love, peace,
my son and daughter,
a lioness by my side;
maybe then… I'll be in my element?

Sandcastles Yesterday

What am I to do?
My body getting older, fatter, greyer;
I'm ever more injury prone and unfit,
no longer do I get exercise induced chemical highs,
no longer have a family to call my own,
no longer a pride to protect.
I wait,
contemplate,
what is light and,
can it be lighter?
Context, everything.

Is lighter referring to a colour,
a mood,
a weight…
or an inanimate object that starts a fire?

If something can be lighter…
can it also be heavier or darker?
or, it's the darkness that enables you to see the light?

I don't want to contemplate,
life hesitate,
but wonder what the next minutes,
hours and months will bring-
fame and fortune?
A broken heart and distressed spirit?
Fight turning to flee?

This revision,
mental collision is my life indecision,
my search for solace,
my retreat,
introspection numbed by alcohol and drugs.

Who am I?
What am I to do?
I, no longer a free-spirited sandcastle boy

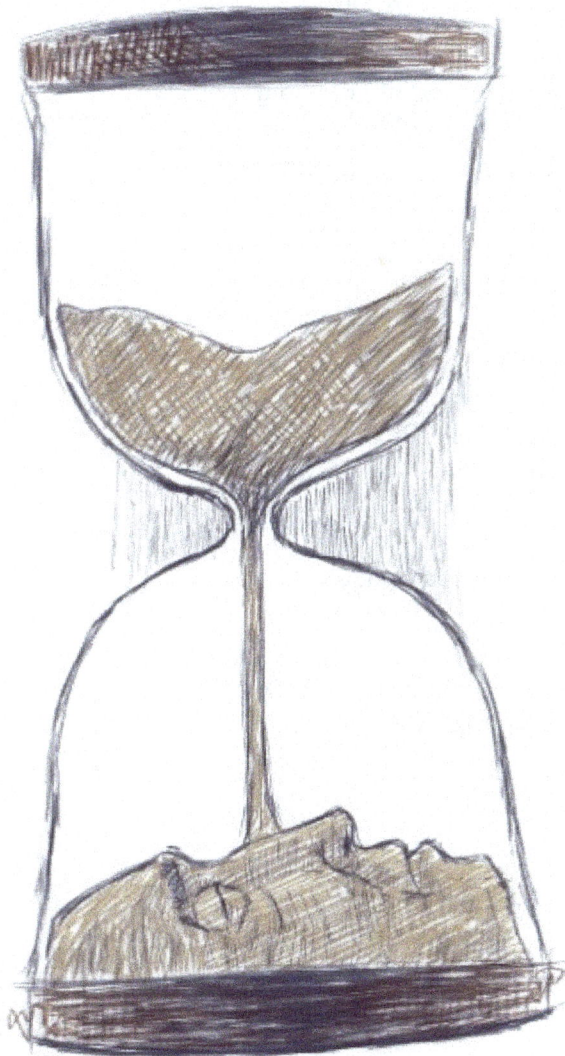

Anticipation

You wait in anticipation for the unfolding of the future,
when minutes seem like days and seconds hours.

Feeling the heat from the skin of your lover.
Smelling the leather in your new car.
Getting dressed for the night that is to follow.
The first day at your new school or job.

Waiting in the hospital delivery room,
to hold your new born son or daughter.
Watching the referee put the whistle to their lips.
Hearing the first crack of gunfire.

What the imminent future holds,
you can't know.
You guess based on experience,
your sixth sense as your body tenses or
relaxes in anticipation,
your senses going into overdrive.

Do you fight or take flight?
Do you run into the maelstrom,

ride up the valley of the shadow of death…
or hide under covers?
Those who harness the power of anticipation
are sometimes called heroes,
those who can't – cowards.

Life is not that simple,
it's never black and white;
everyone has different expectations of what to
anticipate.

How you embrace anticipation says who you are,
though not who you'll be.

Caged Parrot

I'm sitting on a bench,
it's raining,
I'm chatting with a chick I met,
a nice lass from Argentina,
my age,
creative,

She has a joie de vive that's missing from my life,
that I want,
a freedom of mind that I desire,
to be who I am and do what I want,
no consequences,
living life as it should be,
on a whim,
instinctive,
not worrying about today or caring about tomorrow,
now,
only now is what's important,
spreadsheets and proposals left on laptop,
boredom and confusion left at home,
this is the real me,
a fee bird not caged parrot,
taking risks and catching experiences.

She is someone who's fun,
lively,

inspirational,
the aphrodisiac missing from my hum drum life
for five years,
seems forever,
where I neither excite or disappoint,
don't live my ikigai,
have little passion,
meraki,
no longer finding sisu to turn the world on its axis,
where anything is possible,
I, now a caged parrot not free bird.

Emotional Flak Jacket

You enter and leave this world alone,
your choice who joins the journey.
Be by yourself,
make the conscious decision to know no one.
will loneliness, so that rejection becomes impossible.

If no one knows you,
they can't leave you;
you can't be disappointed or let down
by friends or lovers that don't exist.

Being alone,
does not mean always being lonely;
it's not the friendless way,
but the road with less hurt.

Accept solitude rather than risking hope.
Be conservative not proactive.
Hide in the light so you can't touch, hear, feel,
or love someone else…
this way, nothing and no one can destroy you.

I say, put up your barricades,
man the defences,
put on a suit of armour and don a flak jacket for
your soul…
but is this the real me?
I'm a lover not a hater,
so can I,
should I give it up or risk another broken-heart?

Tough Day at the Office

A day like any other,
the sum rising,
moon waning,
the motion of the ocean constant,
the change,
me,
what I know,
my reality,
I,
having expectations,
pray turn to realizations.

Morning turns to afternoon,
joy to despair,
opportunities to disappointment,
hope to hopelessness,
positivity to negativity,
this my new reality,
constant banality,
futility,
all I have left,
durability,
this not liveability,
constant calamity,
what the fuckability
too much miserability,
every day,
a tough one at the office.

Tomorrow,
a day like any other,
the sum rising,
moon waning,
the motion of the ocean constant,
the change,
me,
what I know,
my reality,
I,
having expectations,
need to turn into realizations,
this my invincibility!

Free Bird

I don't need drugs,
other than the love pill,
the anything is possible solution,
the, who you meet and where you go smack;
I'm a free bird,
don't try to keep me caged.

I don't need to be mashed,
smashed,
flying, other than to meet like minds,
those who see the world as a rainbow of unending
possibilities;
I'm a free bird,
don't try to keep me caged.

Always on the move,
from early days to grey beard,
so tie me up,
knots and whips not emotional strangulation;
I'm a free bird,
don't try to keep me caged.

I like free birds,
we,
breaking from the norm,
the 9-5 not for us;
we are free birds,
don't try to keep us caged.

I'm not a rich or attractive man,
but someone who can do,
has a free mind,
doesn't set limitations;
I'm a free bird,
don't try to keep me caged.

I have my life responsibilities,
too often feel like commodities,
why do you want to trap me?
I'm a free bird,
don't try to keep me caged.

I break the rules,
make the rules,
won't listen to your rules,
society or cultural rules;
I'm a free bird,
don't try to keep me caged.

Love me or hate me,
I am me,
a free bird;
don't try to keep me caged.

DESPERATION

In today's supposedly enlightened times, why is suicide increasingly the preserve of men? Likewise, addictions, fighting, disappearing – all male dominated. It begs the question: what is it about modern life that's so discouraging, depressing for men? Why do we, as men, bottle up our emotions? Why can't we feel comfortable in showing our vulnerability and admitting mistakes? Why do we suffer in silence with depression and anxiety?

The are many complexities of modern life and we receive manifold messages on any given day, whether they be government health warnings, the expectation to buy a house or, drink from fancy coffee shops. Also, how, where and when we should be happy; there's a constant stream of conflicting information. Modern life is as complicated as deciphering what being a man means, the two intricately intertwined. It can at times be very difficult to find a reason for being, this itself can lead to desperation, a sense of hopelessness, rising rates of suicide, addiction and a male mental health crisis.

Depressing Memories

There are highs in life...
but more lows.

I've been to many weddings...
and been divorced.

The joy of pregnancy...
becoming miscarriage,
still birth,
abortion.

The greatest job,
the answer to all financial problems...
turning into dreaded retrenchment.

A holiday romance...
leading to a visit at the clinic.

My castle, my home..
until it went into negative equity,
reposed.

The love of a puppy...
is not as strong as the emotion at the death of
man's best friend.

The fitness drive,
pushing my aged body…
ends in premature injury.

Life is full of hope,
only to be dashed again and again,
taken away with the swipe of a pen,
lack of conscience,
stupidity,
karma.

Letter of Despair

Why did you leave?
Why did you vanish without a word or note?
How could you disappear from my life?

As a teen,
I rebelled against mum,
I wanted to be my own man,
to forge an identity out of your shadow.

You were my hero,
my god,
I worshipped at your altar,
your words were my command,
my actions were to please you.

I want my own family,
to be a father,
to not copy your mistakes but make my own.

To live my life…
but with your guidance;
you took that from me.

You were the rock,
the centre of our family.
You gave mum warmth and strength,
advice and direction to my brother,
a joke to cheer me up or shoulder to cry into.

You were larger than life,
everything to us.
You had an answer to every question,
a solution to any problem.

I was afraid to write this poem,
this an ode to you,
my lost father,
the man who walked out on us,
me.

I blamed mum,
caused her such pain,
she always forgiving my recklessness,
ungratefulness
selfishness.
she,
shielding me from the truth.

I don't blame you,
we all have demons.
You are still my god,
my hero,
I just want to understand,
why?

Vortex

I'm unemployed,
desperate for work,
to feed my family,
enjoy life;
I get handouts but want a hand up.

I've brought this on myself.
I'm accountable for my choices so don't feel sorry
for me;
help if you want,
everyone needs a little kindness.

I don't have many friends
those I call such,
I can't trust.
We hang around the bookies,
the casino,
in the park with our cans;
this is not living.

I've brought this on myself.
I'm accountable for my choices so don't feel sorry
for me;
help if you want,
everyone needs a little kindness.

I have a family but not one that lives for me,
loves me,
but rather disowns me.
They won't come to my shithole flat,
they pretend they don't have a father;
I can't blame them,
I fucked everything up.

I've brought this on myself.
I'm accountable for my choices so don't feel sorry
for me;
help if you want,
everyone needs a little kindness.

I screwed up what was good,
my life one of regrets,

thinking what I should have done differently.
My mental health is disintegrating,
I, reliving that moment,
that time in life when I had it all and threw it away.

I've brought this on myself.
I'm accountable for my choices so don't feel sorry
for me;
help if you want,
everyone needs a little kindness.

It should have been the happiest of times,
the greatest of times...
the birth of our third,
but joy turned to grief,
grief to anger at this unjust world,
this world that is utterly incomprehensible.

I've brought this on myself.
I'm accountable for my choices so don't feel sorry
for me;
help if you want,
everyone needs a little kindness.

My love,
my wife,
rejected life
rejected me as she descended into the funk of
depression;
I alone in grief and didn't know how to cope.

I've brought this on myself.
I'm accountable for my choices so don't feel sorry
for me;
help if you want,
everyone needs a little kindness.

Instead of being there for my dear,
my kids,
I withdrew.
Drinking led to flirtation,
desperation to prostitution,
drug experimentation,
anything to forget.

I've brought this on myself.
I'm accountable for my choices so don't feel sorry
for me;
help if you want,
everyone needs a little kindness.

That was five years back.
I was not,
am not a bad man;

I was in a terrible downward spiral...
mind, body and soul caught in a vortex,
I no mental gortex,

I've brought this on myself.
I'm accountable for my choices so don't feel sorry
for me;
help if you want,
everyone needs a little kindness.

I have hope of reconciliation,
of starting life again,
of being reborn into world of the living,
Will you help me?

I've brought this on myself.
I'm accountable for my choices so don't feel sorry
for me;
help if you want,
everyone needs a little kindness.

Breath of Fresh Air

It's been days,
weeks,
months and years in this city,
job,
relationship,
uncertainty,
friendship,
way of life,
one of utmost strife.

I need change,
a breath of fresh air,
new scenery,
to be proactive not reactive,
my mental health in turmoil,
the victim of procrastination;
my waistline,
the victim of drinking to destruction.
my declining bank balance,
continue searching for the party,
happiness,
love,
a sense of being,
camaraderie,
not feeling alone in this fantastical,
unfuckingstandable world where plans go to shit,
hearts are broken,
only serendipity saving me in this life less ordinary,
I, with no company to share a laugh with.

I have forgotten what a warm body feels like,
as,
frustration building,
my dreams only fantasizing,
not realizing,
this not a life worth living,
no body joining,
soul uniting.

I'm human and need more than self.
I hate my jealousy of others enjoying,
exciting,
reuniting.

What's the point of me?

I'm not happy,
won't compromise to solution,
delaying the inevitable,
irretrievable,
kidding myself,
hoping for change,
but not being the change-maker.

I need to break the stick,
finding something,
someone significant,
not be contained,
constrained,
constipated by self-imposed,
culture imposed,
legally enforced limitations.

This is a mad way to live,
this not survival,
not thriving,
living to the limit,
excelling but living in a shoe box.

Options,
no good ones.
This hell is the antithesis of life,
living;
I have to find the surface and breathe fresh air.

Struggling

My father gone,
old and ill,
his time months,
years ago.

A relief,
the man of generous soul,
life of the party,
no longer screaming in pain,
seeing the sadness in my mother's eyes.

Dad was…
friend during friendless teenage years,
a rock for his family,
an example of who a leader is,
he, not needing to be shouty,
alpha through deeds not noise as he went about
life his way,
doing not excusing;
but, he is gone,
his time now.

His pyjamas and tat from around the globe gone
as his memory lives on,
his example of calm in the storm,
my abiding memory as I live thru hurricane times.

Like my pa,
my wife also gone,
emotionally for a long time,
soon to be physically.

Divorce papers written up,
our paths diverging,
kids caught in the maelstrom of mis-understand-
ing,
lack of empathising,
marriage exploding,
work contracting,
kids screaming –
how do I pay the rent?
I'm cut to the bone,
need a way out,
break the mental ropes before I'm dragged under,
to once more live with hope.

This,
a tough moment-
which way to turn?
Friends,
they a friendly shoulder,
wife,
an emotional boulder,
life,
a rollercoaster.

Times before I had refuge,
but dad gone,
mum dealing with her things.

I have to get through for my kids,
struggle to the surface and breathe oxygen,
believe the future will open up,
that I will not just survive but thrive,
whether community or desert island for one.

Walking

I'm walking along the street,
the heat,
humidity,
sweat dripping from my nose.

I'm looking for water,
shade,
this easier than finding answers.

And so this is where I am,
a Berlin Saturday,
summer evening,
sunny but chilly,
jumper in rucksack about to come out,
bottle to lips,
want someone between my hips,
someone to hold onto.

I walk the Spree,
hear many accents,
Canadians, Russians and a Syrians,
all foreigners,
in a foreign country,
like me,
I of not fixed mental abode,
wanderer of the globe,
don't know where I'm from or where I'm going.

The noise,
hustle and bustle,
allows me to forget my dark reality,
I want tranquillity,
not to ask,
what's the purpose of my life?

I don't fully know the here,
nor my home.
No loved ones remain,
my ego,
id,
hanging by a thread.

Friends I laugh with,
silly shit can be talked,
but they don't know my pain,
how my life is spinning out of control as the seasons pass.

I live like a raincloud,
my life stuck in time warp with no hope,
too much failure,
challenges can't be overcome.

I make it through the day,
somehow,
doing what I need,
with who I need,
to survive,
what is thrive?

I need a silver living,
a return of mojo,
electricity to make me go,
accelerate or disgrace,
I don't care,
the journey has to be my cocaine,
destination irrelevant.

Time on this planet
my experience,
mainly pain,
a little pleasure,
but why the fuck measure when every day above
ground is a good one.

Devoid

My life devoid of joy,
devoid of life,
as devoid as it can be.

No one understanding,
few caring,
most just passing;
I, a shadow to their lives,
insignificant.

No one would miss me.
Family – no.
Friends – maybe?
My funeral attended by my children only,
they,
the only ones who kept me going…
but they now flying away with my ex-wife,
she making them anger glowing.

I can't allow them to feel responsible for my death,
my mistakes,
my unhappiness;
they are the ones who shine light into my black
life.

This world is but a stage and I'm coming to my
curtain call.
I shall take a toxic cocktail,
not knowing or caring if I see another sunrise.

I don't think there's an all seeing eye in the sky,
an afterlife;
there will be no glorious reruns,
no greatest hits as my life force departs,
rather,
I will turn to dust as worms feast,
my life remembered as one of abject failure, disappointment,
to me as much as those I've known!

Air Pastry Animal

I'm neither nature or nurture,
culture or tradition,
I am who I am,
a mix of ethics and morals,
loves and hates,
many constituents into the reason of my being.

No one tells me how to live-
not my teacher,
my church,
my family or friends though listen to all,
respect,
agree to disagree and then decide to be the best or
worst of all of the above,
none of the above,
like you,
you who made me,
as much as me,
who made I,
I,
a Spanish omelette of fine ingredients,
the end result,
the sum of the parts greater,
tastier than individual influences.

Confused?
you,
as much as I!

I smoke to find,
drink to think,
whore to explore my being,
my reasoning,
understand my life force.

I can't always find,
so I drink some more.
I can't find,
so imagine and the dance continues,
a whirlwind between possibility and impossibility,
satisfaction or nothing,
no middle-ground,
so drink and smoke more,
more to contort,
to be interesting,
to be a dancing,
waving Chandra,
an air pastry animal.

I, who needs acceptance to be me,
doesn't know where is my life or what's it for.
No one gives a damn,
no one will care when I fall over the edge.

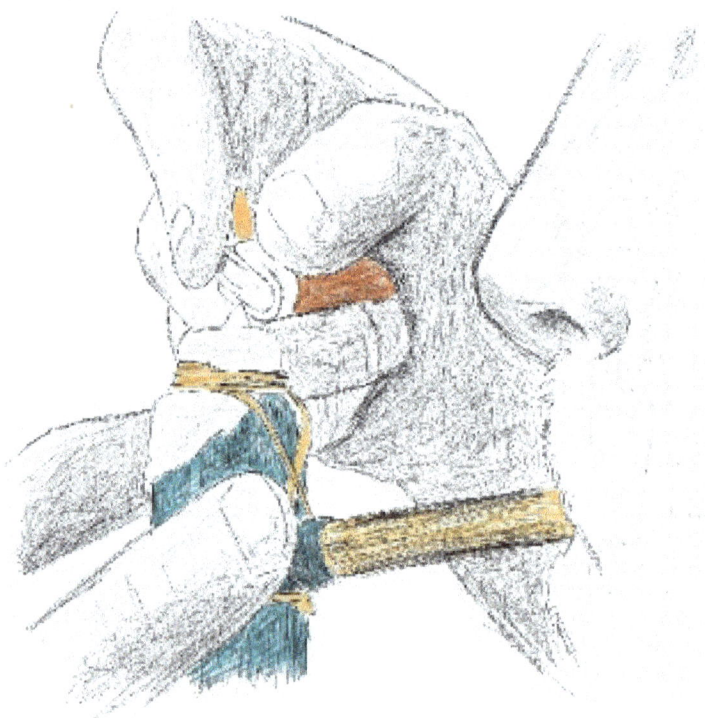

Rejection

I'm in a bar doing my usual,
a night on the beer,
meet friends old and new.

Between the chatter,
I drunkenly gesticulate about how love feels
through the ups and downs,
roundabouts of life,
this I contemplate together with the hate from my
former mate-
now want love to percolate,
tonight,
hopefully copulate.

I look around,
people observe,
each in their own world doing their own thing.
Sometimes friends,
at others, colleagues,
occasional lone wolfs doing their thing,
not caring what others think,
just what's good for them for now.

Back to my present,
reality,
so many beautiful girls around,

mind abound,
head working overtime mentally undressing,
wished caressing,
my heart palpitating,
dick-twitching.

But can I
will I,
should I try my luck or will hope be replaced by
rejection?
Is it better to wet dream than rejection?
No matter the erection,
I can't handle more female rejection.

Drowning

I walk a street of lights,
this not Paris or London,
Tokyo or Cape Town,
but a red light district.

My mind is split
as much as I want to split a woman.
I'm denied fun and frolics by a jealous wife,
trouble and strife,
life,
fate finding me here by myself,
horny and sad,
feel like I'm going mad.
When I laugh to pass the day,
appear gay,
these are tears of a clown,
I, a sad,
lonely,
increasingly grey individual.

Life is passing me by,
no soulmate by my side,
false expectations the price of happiness,

to please others rather than myself,
I,
praying at the altar of life decisions,
those I'm glad of and others I regret,
prefer to forget as I try to make it through to another sunrise,
each disappointment,
each argument making it harder,
more larder,
more,
fuck, what's the next move?

I, no more the smooth operator,
just about head above water,
mentally drowning,
coughing and splattering,
killed from inside out,
I need to shout,
scream,
pull the house down,
stamp on it and burn it to ashes—
maybe only then will a phoenix rise.

Soul Sucked Dry

My soul has been sucked dry,
nothing excites as I go through motions,
need new life potion.

Where once there was passion,
highs and low,
now I'm not enthused,
don't give a shit!

This, is not the real me.
Work, boring.
With friends, boring.

Late nights I don't bother anymore but instead
brood,
wallow in self-pity for the life that's passing me by.

What's there to live for if life is a blank canvas and
you have no paint or brushes?

I have nothing but questions:
Jealousy,
why do you sit on my shoulder?
Money,
why do I chase you?
Alcohol,
why are you my crutch?
Wanderlust,
why can't I be happy with what I have?

I'm zombiefied,
uneventful hours and days pass as I wait for
calamity,
catastrophe,
something to strike a new reality,
anything to shock me out of stupor.

UGLY THOUGHTS

There is no way I can control what third parties do. I can't control a drunk driver hitting me with their car or some crazy chick telling my wife that I'm screwing her. I can't even control my own body, the chemicals going around my noggin deciding if I want pasta, chocolate, vodka or pussy. Other molecules decide if I will be ill or healthy, if my fag-smoking and booze-drinking will lead me to an early grave or I'll live to 100. As such, I think it's understandable to feel a sense of frustration and powerlessness when faced with the unpredictable nature of life and being depressed about it being outta my control.

The only thing I have true control over, is, accepting I'm not in control. If I can master this state of mind, be at one with Gaia, then it might just be possible to live a happy life, have a sense of peace and reduce the impact of disappointment. But, if I can't, then I can control my mind with ugly thoughts. By preparing myself, I reduce the impact of something, someone or somewhere serendipitously turning bad for me.

Is it a sense of shame for not living to the male ideals I'm fed continuously that makes life so incomprehensible? I feel as if I've no control and especially when it comes to women. The feminist movement seems to drive the narrative of male happiness… and this is how Andrew Tate and the incel movement jumped in by saying, don't be ashamed of being a straight white man. You don't need to feel guilt for simply being you. That being a man is great and toxic masculinity is a fabrication of wokedom. He does not represent who I am. True feminism empowers individuals and challenges harmful gender norms rather than diminishing or controlling the happiness of men.

Enlightenment in a Candle

I'm here –
I don't know why,
but I am.

I've met a brown skinned brother who told me
about his country,
a cross dresser who lives life honestly,
students who saw through my sunny façade.

What would happen if I died?
I mournfully think.
A full-stop at the end of life,
the final curtain,
no more reruns,
only greatest hits as I go up the final tunnel.

No one would miss my mistakes,
my unhappiness;
there's no one to shine light into my black life.

I could take a toxic cocktail,
not knowing or caring if I see another sunrise,
where the world is a stage,
I, coming to my curtain call,
the court jester,
mine the tears of a clown.

And then I see a candle.

I look into the flame,
peer into my soul,
try to find deeper meaning.

The candle is flickering,
shining while it still can,
soon to go out like my life –
the course,
run,
extinguished.

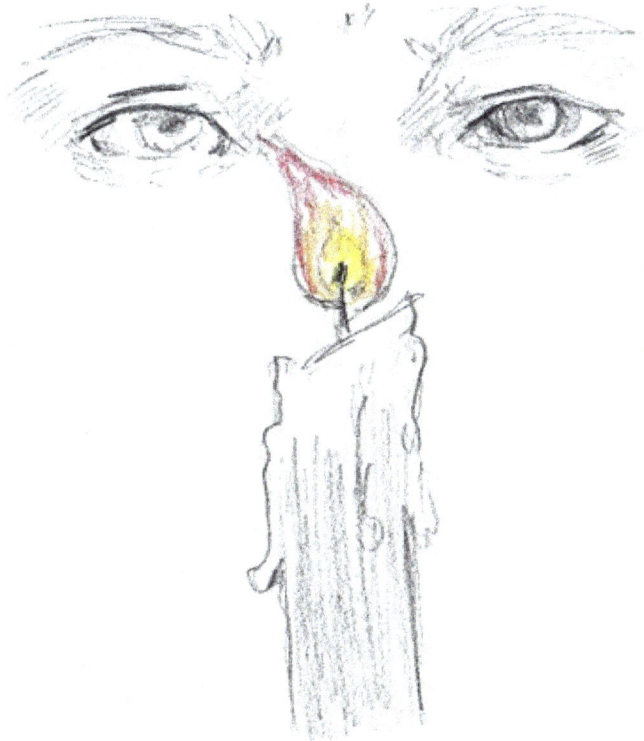

The Murderer

My little red helpers,
my pharmaceutical friends,
drowsy at the wheel,
an unreported hit and run,
I, the runner running from murder.

I drink my drink,
smoke my joint a freeman.
My conscience confused,
my brain beating my skull,
my heart heavy…

Bullshit!

Who am I kidding?
My soul is exhilarated,
the biggest rush in my life,
I'm electrified out of depression.

If I've done it once…
can I do it again?
Should I chase the adrenaline,
but this time not manslaughter and run,
but premeditated hit and slow jog?

What will I feel when I watch the victim twitch…
before engaging reverse?
I'll look into their eyes,
see their final seconds,
their pleading for redemption,
before hope fading into inevitability,
submission as they walk into the valley of the
shadow of death.

I leave the house and start the engine.
Should I turn left to the police station and clear
my conscience,
drive forward to the pharmacy with my prescrip-
tion,
or right to a night of death?

I turn right.

Depression lifted,
murder on my mind,
I wait for an opportunity.

Should I attack with car,
rape or go vigilante?
Decisions, decisions,
glorious decisions.

My alter ego in control,
nothing can stop me;
I'm invincible,
I'm God and tonight I decide fates.

I Am

Who am I and where am I on my life journey?
A point on the time space continuum,
the reincarnation of an ant or a Pharaoh's cat?

How I see myself,
what does that mean?
If you want to get confused,
be confusing.

Divorced wife,
lost daughter,
dead son,
parents abdicating their responsibilities,
brother by rope,
death my only lifeline.

Everything can be mended,
even broken hearts,
broken souls.

Win the lottery,
job interview,
hear from a lover,
control others to lose control of yourself.

Death,
the anaesthesia to love.
Stronger than a band aid,
a tourniquet to life,
where nothingness means as much as something
to drones.

I know the reality of life.
There's no grey beard in the sky to save you,
no afterlife.
You will turn to dust,
worms will feast;
this is the meaning of life.

Everyone fucks others so I'll fuck the motherfucker!
Be an enigma to others and myself,
to control destiny,
to finish a life,
decide fates,
life and death;
that is being God.

I am GOD

I AM SURROUNDED BY THE LIGHT OF GOD
I AM ENFOLDED BY THE LOVE OF GOD

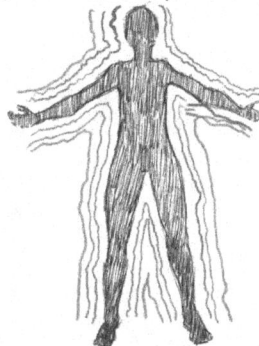

I AM PROTECTED BY THE POWER OF GOD
I AM MELDED WITH THE PRESENCE OF GOD

WHEREVER I AM
GOD IS

2p Machine

Ever since I was small boy,
and now needed more than ever,
pushing coins into a slide-machine has left me
transfixed.

Watching the coppers bounce down to the shelf
that's moving mesmerically,
coins teetering on the edge waiting to be pushed
over the cliff.

I used to pray to the god of gravity as spheres
cascaded onto the lower shelves,
the prize,
a pound or key-ring hanging precariously over the
abyss.

It's slow motion,
the coins splayed,
forwards and backwards they went,,
like life,
never stopping.

Then I would push two down simultaneously,
the machine gobbling them up as they fell over the
sides,
this an analogy for my life.

Murder

I am in the here and now,
not what I was expecting,
hoping,
but it is what it is,
living.

Choices few,
accept the fuck-up,
move on and rebuild or give up.

I am who I am and won't take a step back.
I will swallow and spit out disappointment,
fuck you misgivings,
screw you regrets,
up your ass calamities.

No, this is life,
there is only one.
I will make a decision,
not afraid of the consequences,
good or bad,
I will just do it,
live,
love.

You accused me of a misdemeanour I didn't do,
would never do,
couldn't even think of doing.

I don't have your cunning,
I wouldn't give such final judgement to a person,
a human like me,
good and bad,
strong and weak,
hopeful and challenged as much as I.

All struggle trying to make it through life one day
at a time,
keeping grim psychology at bay,
resisting the urge to use hammers and machetes,
guns and knives on those who wronged us,
bedevilled and made us feel small,
humiliated and tormented,
thought of as lab rat to play with...

But this beast has teeth and claws,
a whip tail and AK-47,
I will prowl the office floor,
the student dorm,
gymnasium and concert hall seeking revenge for
insults,
for being taken for a fool,
an idiot.

Well,
who's smiling now?
You're dead,
lifeless,
I running in the wilderness,
free,
alive.

Suicidal Thoughts

The definition of insanity:
doing the same thing but expecting a different
outcome.

I must be insane as I wake,
shit, shave and shower;
a new day…
yet more calamity.

I'm alive but feel dead,
a corpse with emotions,
a cadaver that can still jig.
Life, full of ups and downs…
death more straightforward.

I accelerate towards an emptiness of my soul.
With no religion,
my belief 40% proof or boiling spoon;
I'm locked onto death,
my future a black hole.

Trying to keep it together,
Mind-rumbling,
will not let it split;
heart-breaking,
thinking of all the shit.

I am now more bad than good,
less exciting,
all sad,
each day depressing.
excruciating,
self-reflecting.
wondering and wandering into the morrow.

Life,
I don't know,
no longer living by my pants,
plenty of bants,
being a game-changer,
life-maker,
now, I'm engine-staller.

Would suicide be a more honourable option,
a clean way to stop the suffering of those closest
to me?
Can my final act be to protect those I love?

My passing will be soon,
my blood deepening the soil.
I will go back from whence life grows,
in the earth I will germinate and complete the
cycle of life,
this,
the only good thing I've done in my miserable
time on earth.

I Walk

I walk the streets at night,
beer and women on my mind.
I walk the mountains,
exercise and loves never forgotten.
I walk the forest,
smelling the alpine air.
I walk the beach,
remembering my childhood.

As I walk,
pebbles between toes,
I think of what might be,
of children building sandcastles.

I walk the aisle,
ex-wife in bridal gown.

I walk the tiles,
to the bathroom,
to my destiny.

I walk cobbled streets,
the perfect analogy for the unevenness of life.

I walk down office steps,
humiliated.

I walk the hospital grounds,
tears streaming down my face,
my boy walking towards his final light.

I walk through life,
memories never lost.

I walk to the doctors
hoping it's just the flu.
I walk towards a gravestone,
coffin in my arms.

I walk to the cabinet,
I open it,
unscrew the bottle top,
open mouth,
deposit.

I walk peacefully through the valley
of the shadow of death.

EMBRACE THE SUCK & MOVE FORWARD WITH A POSITIVE MINDSET

You're amazing! You possess an incredible spirit! These are words I never thought I'd hear another human say to me. Likewise, everything is possible. Never take a setback as the final answer; it is just one more step to reach your goal. Find those people, family, friends, lovers, therapists who can look past your blemishes, imperfections, mistakes, and recognise that only the future truly counts. And, I'm not talking about false bullshit! It's important to hear brutal truth… but as long as this leads to a positive final outcome.

To err is human,
to forgive, divine

Happiness is within everyone's grasp. Everybody can shine if only they afford themselves the chance. The past is just that. No one else is going to get you out of the shit other than yourself. Others may help and support, but ultimately it's your life. So don't blame everyone, and why should God hear your prayers. Find someone who will not judge your past or dictate your future. Admit your weaknesses as then you can start to find solutions. Know and embrace your self-worth. Understand, that each person has the power to shape their own future, this the ultimate responsibility lies with you. Don't expect perfection in others; it's the rough edges that make us who we are and define our uniqueness.

Have the balls to say, screw this, and then try your luck elsewhere. Somewhere, doing something, where you can be a big fish in a little pond as opposed to a scampi in the ocean of fate with little influence over your destiny, flotsam continually being flushed down the lavatory of life. Remember, a vacation won't make things better. Changing jobs or receiving the recognition you deserve won't automatically bring improvement. Drugs aren't a lasting solution. The only thing that will make things better, genuine improvement, lies in nurturing the relationship with yourself.

Restart

What's the worse.
absolute nightmare,
complete mother-fucker where options are zero,
the best,
disaster,
emotional rollercoaster leading to financial calamity,
absolute uncertainty,
most likely end in ruin totality,
is this your reality?
complete mental bestiality,
what was seemed banality,
futility,
now seems livability,
survivability,
but all be down,
broken,
heart stolen,

**RESET
READJUST
REFOCUS
RESTART
AS MANY TIMES
AS YOU NEED TO
JUST DONT QUIT**

so just trying to find a way,
should I go or stay,
last resort…
pray as life falling apart,
all I can do…
restart!

Sisulla Siitä Selviää

I'm faced with challenges,
obstacles physical and mental too big for one person,
one mind to overcome,
that are disproportionate to my experiences,
resources and abilities.

But with sisu,
sisulla siitä selviää-
with me in charge,
anything can be done,
this, I remind myself.

If I can dream or think it,
then I can and will do it.

I will start with the end in mind,
consider all the challenges I've to overcome,
of everything that I've already accomplished!

The times I failed six times…
but made it on the seventh!

Failing is inevitable,
a part of life-
it is the getting up that differentiates the winners from losers,
achievers from those who give up,
those who have sisu,
who are indomitable and who will try,
try and try again.

Shine

Don't be afraid,
grab the bull by the horns,
the scorpion by the stinger;
take life in your hands,
don't let some motherfucker grind you down.

You are you,
stand up and be proud.
Inflate your chest and give two fingers to any who
doubt.

You are individual,
be the best you can be.
Fuck the doubters and haters,
they are cowards,
you, royalty!

Believe in yourself.
There is no such thing as no –
shine!

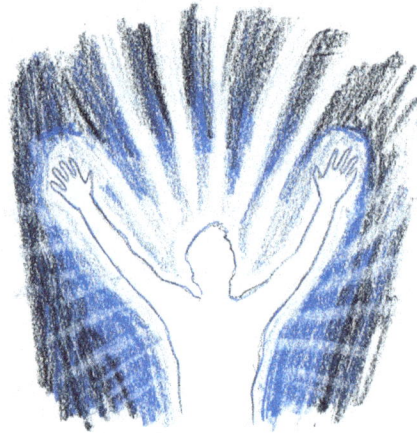

Eye of the Tiger

The rules of life are mine.
Challenges are but obstacles to overcome,
opportunities to be taken advantage of;
nothing can stop me.

Sisu is my indomitability,
meraki my creative soul,
ikigai my reason for being,
my identity.

This is my life and I have the eye of the tiger,
I'm the captain of my pirate ship.

Change is a Coming

As the new year arrives,
so many opportunities,
uncertainties,
fucked-up possibilities.

Change is a coming,
I'm not sure where fate will take me.

I will open doors to my mind,
the day to day;
this is what I need,
who I am.

Change is a coming,
I'm not sure where fate will take me.

I will apply for jobs in far off lands,
new roles in industries unknown,
professional suicide if needed-
I'm not afraid of going back to zero.

Change is a coming,
I'm not sure where fate will take me.

I'll follow my creative passion,
try and turn hobby into income;
I will aim for the moon…
so sure to hit the stars.

Change is a coming,
I'm not sure where fate will take me.

Death is hovering,
family soon to change,
certainties to go,
time for spiritual rebirth.

Change is a coming,
I'm not sure where fate will take me.

Marriage is miserable,
the hardest change of all.
Those've tried so hard for so long,
gone,
what will be my next motivation?

Change is a coming,
I'm not sure where fate will take me.

I will have moon shots,
trust in the randomness of life.
catalyse change,
now is my time.

Change is a coming,
I'm not sure where fate will take me.

As the new day rises,
so many opportunities,
uncertainties,
I love the possibilities,
I will make new realities.

Change is a coming,
I'm not sure where fate will take me,
so I'll plan as if living forever,
but live as if I'm dying tomorrow.

Desperate

My love life is desolate,
a barren wasteland,
a desert with not one flower,
a salt pancake,
a dried sodium lake of lifelessness.

Life is utter dejection,
rejection,
wasted erection,
apathy for the what might be,
could be,
should be,
why the fuck can't it be?

Life is not for me,
I'm listless,
loveless,
meaningless,
hopeless,
friendless and clueless,
knowing my luck,
probably soon to be shoeless.

There is no need to count the number of friends
or size of family when you're alone,
this is the most loneliness,
desperate of expressionless,
emotionless.

You are here in this life on your own,
you arrive and leave this life alone,
you are the only person 100% honest with,
where there are no secrets,
that you can trust fully,

It is only you…
who can experience your version of love,
know your heartache,
feel what it is like to lack acceptance,
as no man is an island,
kids do need parents,
we all need friends for support.

I also need love to get me through the day,
the week,
the year,
life.

I need to be rescued or to rescue,
help or be helped,
love and be loved.

I have much to give.
ample affection,
empathy and downright decency.

I'm a good man who needs a good woman.
I'm done with star signs,
hook-up apps,
watercooler conversations,
supermarket swerves,
friends setting up dates,
perverted prayers and love consultations.

I have reached rock bottom,
more than one occasion I thought I should leave it
all behind,
take the plunge and finish my misery…
and then I saw,
experienced the good,
the positive,
the hope,

the realisation that life is about ups as much as
downs,
plenty roundabouts along the way.

This is our experience,
what it means to be alive.
No matter the bullshit,
the bollocks,
motherfuckers and bullies,
I must find a way to move forward.

For now,
let me live the beautiful lie of happiness.
I will hope in fate
live in the knowledge that the less I search the
more I find.

So, I will take disappointments,
rejection and hate,
this a mindful bridge to the other side,
but, I'll not close my life gate.

In Da Funk

Dad dying,
mum crying,
wife leaving,
kids screaming,
work diminishing-
this isn't living,
barely surviving;
I'm in da funk!

Had tough times before,
but this the gold winner,
truly Olympian the choices have to make.

Things waiting to happen,
living in limbo,
anti-crimbo,
all stress and anxiety,
no joviality,
not sure how,
who,
where,
when,
what will be next.

Dad dying,
mum crying,
wife leaving,
kids screaming,
work diminishing-
this isn't living,
barely surviving;
I'm in da funk!

Life is one of unknowns,
occasionally big moments,
sliding-doors,
events that shape us,
make us who we are,
decide our fate,
we, temporary actors,
players on the global stage.

Dad dying,
mum crying,
wife leaving,
kids screaming,
work diminishing-
this isn't living,
barely surviving;
I'm in da funk!

We have to make the most of time,
life while we have it.
Regrets,
we might have a few,
but hopefully not too many to mention,
so must live each day as if the last-
one day it will be,
this is what I see as I look into my father's dying
eyes.

Dad dying,
mum crying,
wife leaving,
kids screaming,
work diminishing-
this isn't living,
barely surviving;
I'm in da funk!

I see mum's love and fear for her husband,
this, I recognise also in my wife's,
she who will not be with me much longer,
our paths separating,
lives disintegrating the more we cling onto each other.

Dad dying,
mum crying,
wife leaving,
kids screaming,
work diminishing-
this isn't living,
barely surviving;
I'm in da funk!

Work all gone quiet,
this the reality of freelancing,
difficult when look after five,
those who rely on you,
don't understand the mental cartwheels do daily to
keep it together.

Dad dying,
mum crying,
wife leaving,
kids screaming,
work diminishing-
this isn't living,
barely surviving;
I'm in da funk!

Long legal issues,
no book sales,
major things on any other day,
now fleeting thoughts,
nice to have,
not immediate,
compulsory,
life defining,
they, only refining.

Dad dying,
mum crying,
wife leaving,
kids screaming,
work diminishing-
this isn't living,
barely surviving;
I'm in da funk!

Tomorrow the sun will rise,
that's what I remind myself,
convince myself to keep moving forward,
not stalling or going backwards.
Remembering,
this is my life,
strife to be expected,
accepted and overcome;
the greater the challenge,
the more the man revels himself.

Dad dying,
mum crying,
wife leaving,
kids screaming,
work diminishing-
this isn't living,
barely surviving;
I'm in da funk!

I must believe that Sisu will keep me strong,
meraki will help me find creative solutions,
ikigai will remind why I do it all-
this how I will conquer da funk.

I Am a Rainbow

To friends,
I'm red.

To my wife,
I'm orange.

To parents,
I'm yellow.

To children,
I'm green.

To uncles, aunts and cousins,
I'm blue.

To in-laws,
I'm indigo

To colleagues,
I'm violet.

Others see me as a single colour,
but I'm a rainbow,
I am who I am.

I have always been a rainbow,
a kaleidoscope of colours;
if I can't be a rainbow who am I?

Should I be someone I'm not?
Change to fit with what others think I should be,
to conform to expectation but live in misery?

Others see me as a single colour,
but I am a rainbow,
I am who I am.

Life Improvisation

You wake,
go to a job,
chase money,
thinking this will bring happiness,
societal acceptance.

You return home tired,
bored
frustrated,
left wondering,
where did it all go wrong?

You get cultural messages to live happier,
work longer,
social media influence better,
run faster,
vegan muncher,
porn star harder,
yoga bender,
muscle pumper,
Buddhist meditator...
this makes you anxiety sufferer,

lone drinker,
drug abuser,
no friendlier.

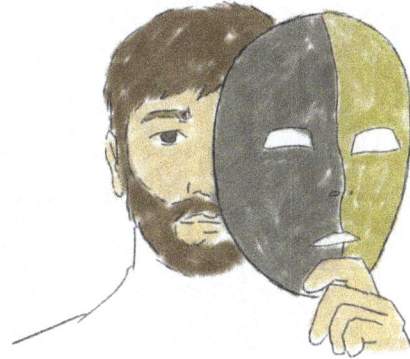

Transform your thinking beyond dynamic.
Become loose in the mind,
extrovert in your creativity,
spontaneity,
serendipity,
all the world an improv stage,
you the lead actor,
the god who designs destiny.

Continue On

I walk,
no destination in mind,
no person to see,
no objective to reach or goal to score,
just wanderlusting,
wondering,
trying to work out who I am,
what I'm doing,
where I'm going,
how I'm getting there and who I'm travelling with,
as I've got people to talk,
the street to meet and mental furniture rearrange.

I may hit the restart,
try over,
be my true self-
not afraid of rejection,
ejection,
but search for life affirmation,
connection.

I will walk the road less trodden,
sodden,
bumpy and enjoy the pain.

I will be a free bird,
not locked,
life shell-shocked,
but love,
live and go large.

Mind Toaster

What a day,
a complete disaster,
rollercoaster,
mind toaster.

Started sunny,
ready to hit the street,
looked fly,
fashionable,
nothing can stop me,
roast me or get in my way.

I'm full-steam pumping,
soon to be Rick Rossing,
James Bond firing,
profit making.

But then....

A blast from the past,
insecurities destroying confidence,
why did I...
a weak individual...
think I could overcome history,
to make destiny and not be ruled by it?

Who can change fate?
Who can challenge the gods?
Is mine not a life predetermined?

These thoughts pass through my brain,
mind drain,
hundreds percent can't constrain,
it's too much pain.

I pause,
take two steps back,
looked at the plain truth of life,
remembered Gloria Gaynor,
and realise,
I am who I am!

I'm neither nature or nurture,
culture or couture,
all the above,
none of the above.

I am who I am,
a mix deciding my ethics,
love and hates,
the reason for being.

No one tells me how to live or love-
not my teacher,
my church,
my family nor friends.

I will listen,
respect,
agree to disagree,
and decide…
to be me,
the best and worst of my reality,
of you,
you who made me,
as much as me who made I,
I,
a Spanish omelette of good ingredients,
the end result tastier even if you don't know why.

Confused?
you as much as I,
but nothing will get in my way,
today,
I, the captain of my pirate ship.

Fuck Your Shit

I've compromised my soul for you...
but it's still not enough;
you always want more and more;
fuck your shit!

I try and try to make you happy,
but you give me nothing in return,
no happiness or thanks,
no value add;
fuck your shit!

Work is tiresome and bollocks,
And for what,
money?
something which I get no benefit from;
fuck your shit.

Getting screwed by lawyers,
unethical motherfuckers,
don't blame me when they reap what they sowed!
I'm going to fuck-up their shit.

I'm no longer going to be a victim of jealousy,
nepotism,
bullying and hate;
fuck that shit!

I have hopes for a lighter tomorrow,
brighter tomorrow,
of living,
perspiring for what I want to achieve.

I will get my shit together,
be the change-maker,
rainmaker to my soul,
captain of my pirate boat the good ship Destiny,
I at her helm,
charting the course out of the doldrums,
inconsistencies and frustrations,
lies and bad relationships to reach the light at the
end of the tunnel.

I will leave toxic love behind and take the road less
travelled.
The journey of life,
the rollercoaster that I live,
what has defined me,
will once more be one of joy and hope,
and not constant shit.

Tough Times

Today has sucked;
on a score of 1 to 10...
I miss the scale by miles!

But, every day above ground is a good day,
I remind myself of that.

My dad,
deathbed few weeks ago,
out of hospital now,
but shit himself,
I clean him up.
This is life,
no embarrassment,
feel his humiliation through laughing about it

But, every day above ground is a good day,
I remind myself of that.

My wife,
soon to be ex,
doesn't talk to me,
turning kids against me,
drains bank account,
makes Machiavellian plans.

But, every day above ground is a good day,
I remind myself of that.

Work,
consultancy,

TOUGH TIMES
NEVER LAST
BUT TOUGH
PEOPLE DO.

a life of ups and downs at best of times,
now more unstable than ever.

But, every day above ground is a good day,
I remind myself of that.

Legal issue,
a book in itself,
justice only for certain types,
lawyers abusing trust;
fuck'em,
I'll keep fighting.

But, every day above ground is a good day,
I remind myself of that.

COVID...
you are my respite!
A relative minor inconvenience in life,
something I can disagree with,
rail against.
You symbolize distrusted politics,
disintegrating economics,
societies broken on purpose.

But, every day above ground is a good day,
I remind myself of that.

Every day above ground Is a good day,
I will remember that.
There are new friends to meet,
experiences to have
relationships changed,
smiles to be had and jokes shared.

I live a rollercoaster,
multiple to be precise,
but what goes down finally reaches the bottom
and will go back up;
I will rise like a phoenix,
every day above ground a good'un,
this, what I remind myself.

Kick-Ass

Life,
people,
those you thought friends,
lovers,
partners till the end of days,
let you down,
deceive,
lie,
emotionally and physically abuse you.

You feel worthless,
a nothing,
no good,
a miserable wreck that no one loves.

You get hit,
beaten,
but go back for more,
your insecurities deceiving,
that one day they will love you the way you love
them,
worship them,
their word your command,
their word making you their sexual deviant,
someone you don't want to be…
but you relent,
give in,

anything to feel love,
hear their whisper,
for them to kiss your neck,
lick between your legs,
make you laugh like a love struck teenager,
anything to see them pleased.

That was me,
a male victim of domestic abuse,
she so obtuse
pretending to be damsel in distress,
a wilted flower,
a bunch of other idioms to the authorities,
they seeing through her lies.
Now I have more life scratches than a kitty,
a humongous tiger could inflict.

I got up,
put my boxing gloves on,
told her to shut the fuck up and took control.

My independence kicked her in the balls,
taught her who the real bad ass,
kick ass positive person was and that she should
get outta my life,
that I didn't won't her negativity as I was royalty!

Life can be a Cunt

Life can be a cunt...
now that's a winner winner chicken dinner of a
first line,
this my reflection,
inflection,
not give a damn about rejection,
moral degradation or cultural realisation.

It's been one of those days,
weeks,
all been a bit shit.
Plans missed,
friendships ruined-
just a bit crap.

I need a getaway,
anywhere,
a new scenery,
new reality,
I'm pissed with banality,
disappointments and let downs.

But, fuck this shit;
this is not who I am!

If it sucks,
I will not be the sucker
but the change-up motherfucker,
treeshaker,
rainmaker,
colonel of armies who will invade,
disappointment fade away,
obliterate,
decimate
nuclear decontaminate,
turn the world back to my will.

Shit day,
fogettaboutit;
the mind's not a jail but a free plain of
opportunity.

I will fly like a bird,
soar on eagle wings and not be the scarecrow that
gets shat upon.
The wind will not choose my destination,
I will be the master of the seasons.

I will not give into fate,
hate,
need to regurgitate,
but take life by the scorpion stinger,
bell ringer.
I will make my own destiny,
reputation to be made and successes celebrated,
failures commiserated.

I will lay bloody emotions by the wayside as I
march forward-
guts or glory,
it'll be a fucking good story!

I will determine a way to live,
thrive not just survive.
Think big,
national,
not regional,
local.

The mind,
life,
is not a jail but the start of possibilities!

All I Can

Shattered,
long day at work.
shitty congestion,
kids already sleeping when I get home;
bollocks to this.

Depressing TV supper of salty lasagne,
no veg,
chemical energy drink;
my stomach will have to work overtime.

Watch the headlines,
follow the first story,
slap the side of my head –
discipline.

Tear my weary body to the bookcase.
599 leaves of academia;
screw this, I think but grab the manuscript anyway,
3,000 words needed by tomorrow.

Turn on laptop,
open a new document,
long night ahead...
Prozac and coffee at the ready.

I will sleepwalk into my salvation;
my goal,
my motivation,
my future in sight,
it will be I who proactively climbs towards the
light,
a new life and to be all I can.

A FINAL THOUGHT

I'm actually a glass half-full kinda guy, a true believer that life has a way of making things come good in the end. I've discovered that writing these poems has had a profound positive impact; they have brought me to a happier and more hopeful place. On the other hand, I now realise that holidays, drinking, shagging, drugs, jobs, recognition or a million other things won't make things better until the relationship I have with myself is healthier. I have a newfound realisation of what the essence of living is all about. As Vivian Greene captured perfectly: life isn't about waiting for the storm to pass, it's about learning to dance in the rain. I love this quote. It is a turbulent world and there are constant storms. Rather than being worried and fighting Gaia and the uncontrollable, one should embrace the challenge, solve problems, create opportunities and be self-aware. Maybe, the storm will never pass and so you must learn to dance gracefully in the rain. The words are energising and the analogy of refreshing one's life cannot be overlooked. Remember, each individual should embrace their own identity, this transcending stereotypes but embracing personal growth and emotional well-being. Furthermore, let us not forget, sharing is caring; don't keep you hurts locked inside. Also, try and be a good listener and lend your ears and hearts to others.

Thank you, dear reader, my friend for being on this poetic journey. I hope through my experiences I have given you a new perspective on life. So, I say, never blame your circumstances. A positive mind-set will always lead to a more fortuitous outcome than a negative approach. One should not fear failure; it happens- get up and give it another lash. Don't be ashamed of your mistakes; learn from them. We all screw-up, accept this is part of life. Embrace experience, good or bad; there is always something to be learned. If you don't go after what you want, you will never have it. If you don't ask, the answer is always no. If you don't step forward, you will remain in the same place. Be curious and have a willingness to engage with the unknown. Questioning does not show weakness but is rather a sign of strength, a true measure of intelligence. Open yourself to the world and express that you aren't afraid to exhibit your ignorance but want to learn, search for knowledge and truth from those who can educate and guide. "By doubting we are led to question, by questioning we arrive at the truth." Peter Abelard, 1079- 1142

Keep Walking

As a certain Scottish gentleman once said,
"Keep walking."

Maybe he meant:
keep walking to the off-licence or the bar to im-
bibe his fiery liquid infusion?

Or maybe,
as a way of life?
Keep walking forward,
never take a backward step,
never let someone or something get in your way.

Be yourself,
know your destination.
decide in your direction and keep walking forward.

Hold your head high,
be strong in your conviction and nothing can or
will stop you.

Keep walking can be the anthem of your life.
Never give up,
never stop,
don't let any bastard hold you down.

Always move forward;
keep walking.

BACK COVER BLURB

Embark on a profound journey through the intricate labyrinth of a man's life, where complexity and challenges converge into a bewildering tapestry of emotions. In a world seemingly crumbling around him, he grapples with the recent loss of his father, the initiation of a divorce after a 14-year marriage, a slowing career trajectory, and the relentless ascent of debt, all creating a bleak landscape where great uncertainty looms ominously.

This poignant and unflinchingly honest collection of poems, grouped into themes, encapsulates the male experience in a society influenced by distorted ideals propagated by celebrity culture and social media. The author contends that these unrealistic standards contribute to the male mental health crisis, challenging the limited stereotypes that confine men to emotional stoicism and an exclusive pursuit of physical connection.

Within these verses, you'll witness the raw vulnerability of a man striving to emerge from the depths of despair, embracing his true self, and ultimately finding resilience in the face of the male mental health crisis. His story will shatter taboos, encourage you to confront your own demons and extend a compassionate ear to those in need, and forge a brighter future, one marked by authentic friendships and healing through self-discovery.

ABOUT THE AUTHOR

I'm an entrepreneur & business consultant by day, novelist & poet by night. The son of a British Army officer, I volunteered in rural Tanzania in 1997 before going to university to study marketing. I have lived and worked in Ethiopia, Germany, Kenya, Jordan, Ireland, Malawi, Saudi Arabia, Tanzania and the UK over the last 25 years, my varied experiences of culture, relationships, food, music and everything else that makes the world go round, the source of my inspiration.

www.ingramcontent.com/pod-product-compliance
Lightning Source LLC
Chambersburg PA
CBHW081552040426
42448CB00016B/3299